I Wonder Why

Pine Trees Have Needles

and Other Questions About Forests

Jackie Gaff

KINGFISHER

BOSTON

KINGFISHER

a Houghton Mifflin Company imprint
222 Berkeley Street
Boston, Massachusetts 02116
www.houghtonmifflinbooks.com

First published in 2005
10 9 8 7 6 5 4 3 2 1

1TR/1104/SHE/RNB(RNB)/126.6MA/F

LIBRARY OF CONGRESS CATALOGING-IN-PUBLICATION DATA
has been applied for.

ISBN: 0-7534-5861-6
ISBN: 978-07534-5861-7

Series designer: David West Children's Books
Author: Jackie Gaff
Consultant: Sara Oldfield
Illustrations: Steve Caldwell 4, 5, 14–15; Chris Forsey
24–25, 28—29, 30–31; Elaine Gaffney 8, 8bl;
Neil Reed 10, 11, 12–13t, 13br, 19tr, 22tr;
Peter Wilkes (SGA) all cartoons.

Printed in Taiwan

CONTENTS

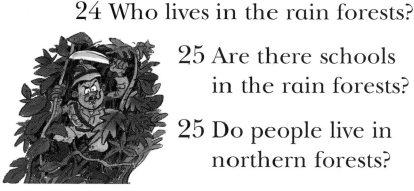

What is a forest?

A forest is a large area of land covered in trees. Beneath the trees there are smaller plants such as bushes and flowers. Living among the plants there are all types of animals— insects, birds, and in some forests bigger creatures such as foxes or wild boars.

● A single tree in an oak forest is home to as many as 400 types of animals, from insects and spiders to birds and squirrels.

How do forests help us breathe?

Like other animals, we breathe in oxygen from the air and breathe out carbon dioxide. Trees help us because they take in carbon dioxide and give out lots of oxygen.

● In a single year a forest with 400 trees gives out enough oxygen to keep at least 20 people breathing.

Which forests have the largest trees?

The redwood forests in California have the tallest trees. Redwoods grow to be more than 276 feet (75m)— that's higher than a 30-story building!

● If left untended, almost any field will slowly turn into a forest. Bushes take over from grass and then trees take over from bushes.

Where is the biggest forest?

● Around one third of Earth's land is covered in forests.

Gigantic forests of conifer trees stretch all of the way across the top of Asia, Europe, and North America. The largest of these northern conifer forests is in the Russian Federation in Asia. It makes up one fifth of all the forests on Earth.

NORTH AMERICA

● The largest rain forest is the Amazon rain forest. With an area of almost two million sq. mi. (5 million km²), it covers two thirds of South America.

SOUTH AMERICA

Tropical rain forest—mostly evergreen broad-leaved trees, warm and rainy all year-round.

Tropical dry forest—mostly evergreen broad-leaved trees, drier than rain forest regions.

Temperate broad-leaved and mixed forest—mostly deciduous broad-leaved trees.

● The northern conifer forests of North America,
Europe, and Asia cover almost eight million sq. mi.
(20 million km²)—more than twice the size of the U.S.!

EUROPE

ASIA

AFRICA

AUSTRALIA

Temperate conifer forest—
mostly evergreen conifers,
few deciduous trees.

Northern conifer forest—mostly
evergreen conifers, cool, short
summers and long, cold winters.

Broad-leaved forest and open
woodland—trees more widely
spaced apart than in forests.

What are broad-leaved forests?

Broad-leaved forests are mostly made up of broad-leaved trees—maples, oaks, and other types of trees with broad, flat leaves. The leaves of broad-leaved trees come in all shapes and sizes.

Sycamore

Oak

Maple

Why do some forests go naked in the winter?

Tree trunks and branches are woody and tough, but the leaves of most broad-leaved trees are paper-thin and weak. These leaves are not tough enough to survive during very cold winters. So most broad-leaved trees lose their leaves in the fall, just as we start bundling up against the cold weather.

Trees that lose all their leaves in the fall are called deciduous. Trees that do not are called evergreen. Most broad-leaved trees are deciduous but not all—koalas munch on evergreen broad-leaved trees called eucalyptus trees.

Why do pine trees have needles?

Along with cedars, firs, and yews, pine trees belong to a group of trees called conifers—trees that produce cones. Like most conifers, pine trees do not shed all of their leaves in the fall. This is because the pine tree's needle-shaped leaves are small and leathery—tough enough to survive in the harsh winter weather.

• The smallest conifer cones are not much longer than your thumbnail. The biggest are longer than your arm!

• Crossbills are named after their strangely shaped beak. This works like a lever to help the bird reach the tasty seeds hidden inside conifer cones.

Does it rain in rain forests?

It doesn't just rain, it pours! In these tropical forests rain splashes down almost every day, and there are thunderstorms on as many as 200 days every year.

Why are rain forest trees like umbrellas?

The crowns, or tops, of rain forest trees grow so wide and so thick that they act like umbrellas, stopping a lot of the rain from reaching the ground. They also block out most of the sunlight, making the forest floor murky and mysterious.

● Jungles are the thickest parts of a rain forest. The plants grow so closely tangled together that the only way you can get through them is by hacking out a new path.

Emergent

Canopy

- The crowns of rain forest trees form a rooflike canopy with a few extratall trees, called emergents, poking out above it.

- The crown of a rain forest tree can be as wide as a soccer field is long!

Crown

Liana

Understory

- Giant vines called lianas climb up the tree trunks and dangle from the branches.

- The shady, lower part of the rain forest is called the understory.

- Hidden in the gloom of the rain forest floor are millions of insects such as army ants. These ants don't take any prisoners—they'll eat almost anything they find.

Floor

Why do plants grow in the air?

Many rain forest plants grow high up on tree branches, where they get more light than they would if they grew down on the ground. They are called epiphytes, or air plants, because their roots get the water and chemicals that they need to make food from the air, not the soil.

● Some types of tree frogs can launch themselves into the air to glide from tree to tree.

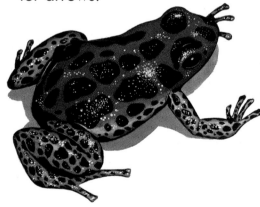

● Poison dart frogs are named because rain forest peoples use the poison in their brightly colored skin as a deadly tip for arrows.

● The bee hummingbird is the world's smallest bird. It is barely two inches (5cm) long.

● The Hercules beetle is the world's longest beetle. Its body is as long as a house mouse's body and tail!

Is the birdwing a bird?

No, the Queen Alexandra's birdwing is the world's biggest butterfly— named because it is bigger than many birds! It lives in rain forests in Papua, New Guinea, and its outspread wings can be a gigantic 12 inches (30cm) across.

Do hummingbirds hum?

These tiny birds are named after the humming sound made by their beating wings as they hover close to flowers, feeding on sugary nectar.

Why do jaguars have spotted coats?

If you have ever walked through a thick forest, you will have seen that sunlight looks spotted as it filters down through the trees. The jaguar's coat helps it hide in this type of speckled light, ready to surprise its prey. It hunts everything from deer and wild pigs to turtles and fish.

● The jaguar is a sneaky hunter. It will dangle its tail in the water like a fishing line in order to attract fish.

How do aye-ayes hunt insects?

The aye-aye has an extralong and extraskinny finger on each hand. It uses these weird fingers to twist inside of insect tunnels and hook out its favorite meal of insect grubs. It lives in the rain forests of Madagascar off Southeast Africa.

● The aye-aye finds insect tunnels by tapping on tree trunks with its extralong finger—and listening out for a hollow sound with its extrabig ears.

One of the strangest-looking monkeys is the proboscis monkey—the word means "long, bendable nose." Proboscis monkeys live on the island of Borneo near the Philippines, where they make their homes in trees close to rivers.

Do spider monkeys spin webs?

No, they got their name because their long, skinny legs, arms, and tails make them look a little bit like spiders. These monkeys are excellent climbers and use their tails like extra hands. They live high up in the treetops of the rain forest.

Howler monkeys are the noisiest rain forest animals. At dawn and dusk troops of them can be heard howling in order to stake their claim to the part of the forest that they call home.

What are cloud forests?

These beautiful, mysterious rain forests grow on the sloping sides of mountains in tropical parts of the world. Wispy clouds cling to the treetops or drift through the branches. The clouds form as warm air rises from lowland valleys into the higher, cooler mountain air.

● One of the biggest banyan trees covers an area larger than 32 tennis courts! Banyans grow in southern Asia—the record holder is in the botanical gardens in Kolkata (Calcutta), India.

Which tree looks like a forest?

A single banyan tree can almost turn into a forest by itself because of its unusual way of growing. Its branches send stiltlike growths to the ground, where they take root and grow into trunks. The new trunks grow new branches, which send out more stilts. And so the banyan tree spreads and spreads!

● The mountain gorilla lives in the cloud forests of Africa. It will often climb into the trees at night to make a cozy nest.

Where do forests grow on stilts?

Forests of mangrove trees grow in muddy waters along tropical seashores. The mangrove also sends down stiltlike roots from its branches. It uses its stilts as props and anchors, not to spread itself out.

● Most tree roots take oxygen from the soil, but it is difficult for mangroves to do this in muddy water. Their roots take oxygen from the air instead—by sending periscope-like growths up from their stilts.

Which are the coldest forests?

Short summers and long, cold winters make the forests that grow in the far north of Asia, Europe, and North America the world's coldest. Only tough trees can survive, so the northern forests are mostly made up of conifers.

● The triangular shape of conifers helps snow slide off of them.

● Wolves will eat any type of animal but the bigger the better. Their favorite meal is reindeer.

Why do reindeer shovel snow?

Herds of reindeer roam through the northern forests. They eat plants and other food that is difficult to find when the ground is covered with snow. Their big hooves come in handy as shovels!

● North American reindeer are called caribou. This is a Native American word meaning "shoveler."

Where do bears go in the winter?

Bears of the northern forests escape the winter chill by snuggling up inside of their dens. They sleep most of the time, living off of the body fat that they built up during the summer.

● Raccoons also sleep through the winter in dens.

Which forests are always changing?

Every season brings changes to deciduous forests and woodlands in temperate climates. Trees are bare in the winter, but in the spring they sprout a fresh green coat of leaves, while bluebells and other flowers form a carpet on the ground. In the fall leaves turn rich colors before falling.

winter   spring

What keeps foxes busy at night?

All sorts of woodland animals live nocturnal lives—awake at night and asleep during the day. Foxes come out to hunt for their dinner as darkness falls. They will eat any small creatures that they can catch.

● Owls hunt at night. Most have good night-time vision, but some have extrasensitive hearing. They can pinpoint prey by the rustling noise animals make scurrying along the ground.

Do woodpeckers eat wood?

No, but they do spend most of their time pecking at it. They do this in order to dig out insects or to hollow out a nest.

summer   fall

● European badgers are also night-time creatures. Their home is an underground den called a sett, and they are very tidy creatures. They often clean out old bedding, replacing it with a fresh supply of grass and leaves.

● Muscles on the woodpecker's head act as shock absorbers, protecting its skull from the motion of drilling.

Where do koalas live?

Koalas are picky creatures. They only eat the leaves and young shoots of eucalyptus trees. So the only place koalas live in the wild is in the treetops of the Australian eucalyptus forests.

● Koalas get water from their food and rarely need to drink. Their name comes from an Australian aboriginal word meaning "no drink."

● Young Australian forest animals, such as opossums (above) and koalas (below), start life in their mother's pouch and then hitch a cozy ride on her back.

● The last place you might expect to see a kangaroo is up in a tree. But that is exactly where tree kangaroos spend most of their lives!

Which is the biggest forest bird?

Cassowaries are shy birds that hide in thick undergrowth in Australia and New Guinea. The largest type can be 5.6 ft. (1.7m) high—as tall as some adults! Cassowaries cannot fly, but they are great runners, and they can swim too!

● The kiwi bird of New Zealand forests cannot fly either. It is also the only bird that is known to have nostrils at the end of its bill.

Who lives in the rain forests?

Many different tribes of peoples live in the world's rain forests. Most build homes in clearings and dig out vegetable patches where they grow their own food. The soil in rain forests is not very good though, and it does not have enough goodness to grow food year after year. After a few months or a few years the rain forest people pack up and move to another clearing.

● Tribal people get all they need from the rain forest, from food to clothes and medicines.

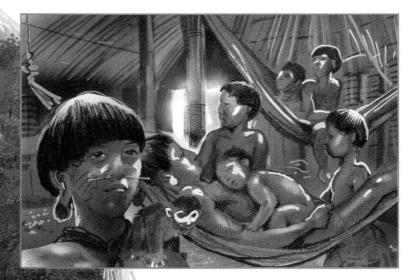

● The Yanomami people live in the northwest of the Amazon rain forest. Several families live together in big round houses called shabonos.

Are there schools in the rain forests?

Few tribal children go to school. Instead their parents teach them how to survive in the rain forest—how to hunt and fish and which plants are good to use as food or as medicine.

● In northern Scandinavia the Sami people make a living by fishing, hunting, and herding reindeer.

Do people live in northern forests?

Yes, the conifer forests of North America, Europe, and Asia are home to many tribes. In Canada, for example, Native Americans called the Woodlands Cree live in forest settlements.

What were the first forests like?

The first forests grew around 350 million years ago. They were made up of tree-sized plants called horsetails and club moss, which looked like giant reeds and ferns.

• Huge insects lived in the first forests, including bird-sized dragonflies.

• Ancient club moss grew to a giant 98 ft. high.

Which dinosaurs lived in conifer forests?

Conifer forests were in existence by the time of the dinosaurs. Only the larger types of dinosaurs, such as *Iguanadon*, were tall enough to munch on conifer leaves.

● When the plants of the prehistoric forests died, they were buried under layer after layer of mud. For millions of years the plants were squashed and squeezed, and they slowly turned into coal.

● Prehistoric insects are often found inside lumps of amber—the fossilized gum of pine trees. Fossils are the stony remains of ancient life-forms.

Which tree outlived the dinosaurs?

The monkey puzzle tree is still around today, even though it dates back to the time of the dinosaurs.

How do forests help doctors?

Forest peoples have known for a long time how to treat sicknesses with plants, and scientists are still studying them. Eucalyptus oil is used in cough syrup, for example, while rosy periwinkle from Madagascar is used to make a drug for treating cancer.

● Around one fourth of the medicines doctors use today come from rain forest plants.

Which foods came from the rain forest?

Avocado, banana, mango, corn, passion fruit, pineapple, and sweet potato all come from plants that were first found in rain forests. So was the cacao tree, which gives us chocolate!

Where do chewing gum trees grow?

More than 1,000 years ago the Maya people of Central America made a sticky discovery about a rain forest tree called the sapodilla— its milky sap makes a chewy gum. It is still used in chewing gums today.

● Rubber, made from the sap of rubber trees, was also found in the rain forests of the Americas. European explorers were amazed to see Native Americans making "shoes" by spreading the sap on their feet!

Why do people cut down trees?

Throughout history people have cut down trees for their wood. Forests are also destroyed in order to clear land for farming or for building towns and cities.

• Wood is used to make everything from furniture and houses to paper, plastic, and soap.

Are forests in danger?

Yes, they are, because too many trees are being destroyed. Tropical rain forests are in the most danger—an area the size of England, Scotland, and Wales is cut down every single year.

What are people doing to save forests?

Conservationists are people who try to protect Earth's precious plant and animal life. Together with some countries' governments, they are working to slow down the destruction of forests and plant new ones.

● The tiger is one of the many animals that are in danger of dying out because their forest homes are being destroyed.

● Some forests are set aside as national parks, where trees are protected and can't be cut down and cleared.

● Each year 1.5 billion tree seedlings are grown in the United States. That's around five new trees for each American.

Index

A

air 5, 12, 17
Amazon rain forest 6
amber 27
animals 4, 9, 11–15, 17, 18–23, 26, 31
ants, army 11
aye-ayes 14

B

badgers, European 21
banyan trees 16
bears 19
beetles, Hercules 13
birds 4, 9, 12, 21, 23
broad-leaved forests 6, 7, 8
see also deciduous, rain forests
butterflies, birdwing 13

C

canopy 11
caribou 19
cassowaries 23
chewing gum 29
chocolate 28
cloud forests 16, 17
coal 27
conifers 6, 7, 9, 18, 25, 26
conservationists 31
crossbills 9

D

deciduous 9, 20
dinosaurs 26

E

emergents 11
eucalyptus trees 9, 22, 28
evergreens 9
see also conifers

F

flowers 4, 12, 20
food 28
foxes 20
frogs 12, 13

G

gorillas, mountain 17

H

hummingbirds 12

I

insects 4, 11, 27

J

jaguars 14
jungles 10

K

kangaroos, tree 23
kiwi birds 23
koalas 9, 22

L

leaves 8, 9, 20
lianas 11

M

mangroves 17
medicine 28
monkey puzzle trees 27
monkeys 15

N

northern conifer forests 6, 7, 18–19, 25

O

oaks 4, 8
owls 21

P

people, forest 24–25
pine trees 9, 27
prehistoric forests 26–27

R

raccoons 19
rain forests 6, 10–17, 24, 25, 28–29, 30
redwoods 5
reindeer 19, 25
roots 12, 17
rubber 29

S

Sami people 25
sapodilla 29

T

tigers 31

U

understory 11

W

wolves 18
wood 30
woodlands 7, 20–21
Woodlands Cree people 25
woodpeckers 21

Y

Yanomami people 24

32